INFINITE
LOVE

30-Day Devotional Journal

Takeelia Carter

A GOSHEN PUBLISHERS BOOK   VIRGINIA

INFINITE LOVE
30-Day Devotional Journal

ISBN: 978-1-7370949-9-9
Copyright ©2021 Takeelia Carter

Library of Congress Cataloging-in-Publication Data

Published in 2021 by:

GOSHEN PUBLISHERS LLC
P.O. Box 1562
Stephens City, Virginia, USA
www.GoshenPublishers.com

Our books may be purchased in bulk for promotional, educational, or business use. For inquiries please contact the publisher via email: Agents@GoshenPublishers.com.

All definitions are original from the author.

All Scriptures are from translations indicated when quoted.

First Edition 2021

Cover designed by Goshen Publishers LLC

Printed in the United States of America

Dearly Beloved,

You are known by God.

You are seen by God.

You are accepted and always and forever loved by God.

Much love and blessings to you as you
walk in your journey

Takeelia Carter

INTRODUCTION

In the beginning of my healing journey, God would have me sit down and write "I AM (BLANK), THAT I AM" quotes and words of affirmations until I could not write anymore. I began to search the Scriptures to find out what the Word of God said about these affirmations that I was declaring and who He said I was. Meditating on these words every day, I began to put these Scriptures on sticky notes, along with goals and the things that I was believing God for, in my dining room area where I worked.

I would read and meditate on them every single day. Once I became free in my affirmations and saw the goals come to pass, I would take them down and replace with more words of affirmation and goals that I was believing God for. Before long, I was walking in those things that I began to declare over my life. Whenever I would get distracted with life and what others would give in their opinions, I would go back to what God said about me. Today, I walk in what and who God says about me and the journey just keeps getting better!

Infinite Love: 30-Day Devotional Journal is a tool to use in establishing or reestablishing your self-love, self-care, self-value, self-worth, and your relationship with God. What does God say about you? Who does He say you are? What were you created for? What is your purpose here on this earth? These are the things that I began to question and discover when I began to walk on my healing journey. It is a daily task to work on self.

This journal is to help you get to a place where it becomes a part of you and your daily life, helping you to discover who you are so that you can begin to walk in purpose. It is said that whatever we do for more than 21-days becomes a lifestyle. Once you get the hang of things, it will become a natural part of your life.

My prayer is for you to discover who you are and your purpose here on this earth. It is to bring you into the awareness of who God says you are. And if you already have an idea or have gotten out of alignment with the Divine, it is to illuminate and get you back to the place of revelation of who He says you are.

My assignment from God is to pass on the healing and teachings that God has given me in helping me to overcome. I hope that once you come to your place, you will be encouraged to do the same. You are blessed to be a blessing!

INSTRUCTIONS

Infinite Love: 30-Day Devotional Journal is a journey into self. Now granted, not everyone is the same and some may need more time to reflect on their daily assignment. No worries! This is to be done and completed at your own pace. Each day is in order with your "I AM" quote to be written and said three (3) times, the definition of that word, the thought behind the word, what you are grateful for that day, the goal for the day, and ending in a prayer to be said aloud. You can also add to that prayer.

The "I AM" quote is to be said and written three (3) times. Say it with boldness and even look at yourself in the mirror as you say it. Besides, you are your best and biggest cheerleader! If you don't believe in yourself, who else will?

The definition of the word is so that you will know what you are saying about yourself. It is important that we know the words we speak over ourselves. Words have POWER! Remember, the power of life and death are in a person's tongue. What you say about yourself is manifested and becomes your reality. So now that you know what you speak, you can say with BOLDNESS who God says you are!

The thought behind the word is to give you an idea of what and who God says you are. It is to encourage you to walk in the fullness. These thoughts are Holy Spirit inspired and influenced.

The goal for the day can be anything. Whether your goal is to start a business, call someone and tell them you love them, make a self -care day, or even just to get out of the bed. Whatever your goal for the day is, write it down and focus on accomplishing that goal. You will find that your goals may increase over time or not. Even if you have multiple goals, if you can accomplish one of them, you did great!

Finally, everything is ended in prayer. You can also add to that prayer or whatever God may put on your heart in reflecting on your daily journey. The purpose is not only to get in tune with self, but also to build a stronger relationship with our Creator.

He is and always has been waiting on you to communicate with Him. He wants to share with you your true identity in Him. He wants to bring you to a place of trust not only in Him but in yourself so that He can bless you beyond your wildest imagination! He wants to bring you into a place of abundance and knowing your identity in Him will help to manifest in His will and power, not yours. This is a relationship built on trust. In trusting Him, you can trust yourself.

Have fun and enjoy the journey!

DAY 1:

"I AM LOVED"

"I am loved" means I am held dearly with a feeling of passion, and tenderness.

Say it and write it 3 times:

1. _____

2. _____

3. _____

SCRIPTURE: John 3:16 (TPT) "For this is how much God loved the world-he gave his one and only, unique Son as a gift. So now everyone who believes in him will never perish but experience everlasting life."

BONUS SCRIPTURE: 1 John 4:19 (KJV) "We love him, because he first loved us."

THOUGHT: God is passionate and His heart is tender toward you. He holds you very dear to His heart. He so loved YOU that He sacrificed His Son Jesus to save you, cleanse you from past, present and future sin and to bring you back into relationship with Him. He is always and forever devoted to loving you.

There is NOTHING in this world that you can ever do to separate you from His love.

WHAT AM I GRATEFUL FOR TODAY?

_____

_____

_____

WHAT IS MY GOAL FOR TODAY?

_____

_____

_____

PRAYER: Father God, I thank you for loving me first. I thank you for loving me no matter what choices I have made that may not align with Your will for my life. I pray that you will shed light on the places that I need your love the most, showing me how you love me in those places. I pray that I will have patience with myself in seeing and loving myself the way that You do. In Jesus' name, Amen.

ADDITIONAL PRAYER:

_____

_____

_____

Day 2:

"I AM ENOUGH"

"I am enough" means that I am adequate and sufficient.

Say it and write it 3 times:

1. _____

2. _____

3. _____

SCRIPTURE: Philippians 4:19 (TPT) "I am convinced that my God will fully satisfy every need you have, for I have seen that abundant riches of glory revealed to me thought the Anointed One, Jesus Christ."

THOUGHT: You are enough and you have enough! You are everything that God needs you to be. Everything that you need is already on the inside of you. It was given when He created you. Do not allow anyone, including yourself to try to convince you differently. There are no inadequacies in Him.

WHAT AM I GRATEFUL FOR TODAY?

_____

_____

_____

WHAT IS MY GOAL FOR TODAY?

_____

_____

_____

PRAYER: Father God, thank you for creating in me enough of all that I need. Thank you for supplying all of my needs before I even know them. When I am feeling inadequate, show me your supply that I may draw from You as my source. I thank you Father for I believe that You created me to be enough and to have enough in every area of my life. In Jesus' name, Amen.

ADDITIONAL PRAYER:

_____

_____

_____

DAY 3:

"I AM ACCEPTED"

"I am accepted" means that I am regarded as right and true. I have favor.

Say it and write it 3 times:

1. _____

2. _____

3. _____

SCRIPTURE: Jeremiah 1:5 (AMP) "Before I formed you in the womb, I knew you [and approved of you as My chosen instrument], And before you were born I consecrated you [to Myself as My own]; I have appointed you as a prophet to the nations."

THOUGHT: God has already accepted you and approved you for the task! You only have an audience of One, "THE ONE". You don't have to please people to be accepted. God has already favored you. This means that you don't have to look for acceptance from anyone. Be who He created you to be and do what He has created you to do without feeling like you need to be understood. God already understands you. The right people will be drawn to you and will understand you, loving you for you. Again, you only have an audience of One and He has already accepted you.

WHAT AM I GRATEFUL FOR TODAY?

_____

_____

_____

WHAT IS MY GOAL FOR TODAY?

_____

_____

_____

PRAYER: Father God, thank you for already accepting me. Thank you that I already have Your approval and don't need approval from humanity. I will not allow the opinions of others to cloud my mind of who You say I already am. I will continue to rely on Your acceptance and not man's opinion. Thank you, Father, for continuing to remind me that I am accepted. In Jesus' name, Amen.

ADDITIONAL PRAYER:

_____

_____

_____

DAY 4:

"I AM A CHILD OF GOD"

"I am a child of God" means that I was born traceable to a cause.

Say it and write it 3 times:

1. _____

2. _____

3. _____

SCRIPTURE: John 1:12 (NLT) "But to all who believed him and accepted him, he gave the right to become children of God."

THOUGHT: When you believed and gave your "YES" to God by accepting Jesus Christ as your Lord and Savior, you became born again in the spirit to our Spiritual Father in heaven. You were adopted into the family of believers, into the Kingdom of God. Being a child of God is your birth right! You belong to the Most High and are promised the inheritance of all that comes with being His daughter.

WHAT AM I GRATEFUL FOR TODAY?

_____

_____

_____

WHAT IS MY GOAL FOR TODAY?

_____

_____

_____

PRAYER: Father God, I thank you for adopting me into Your Kingdom. I thank you that in being your child I lack nothing in You or Your Kingdom. I thank you for giving me the birth right to be Your daughter. I pray that in giving testimony to Your goodness, it will draw others to be adopted into Your Kingdom as believers for themselves. In Jesus' name, Amen.

ADDITIONAL PRAYER:

_____

_____

_____

DAY 5:

"I AM ROYALTY"

"I am royalty" means that I am connected to a royal lineage.

Say it and write it 3 times:

1. _____

2. _____

3. _____

SCRIPTURE: 2 Samuel 7:16 (AMP) "Your house (royal dynasty) and your kingdom will endure forever before Me; your throne will be established forever."

THOUGHT: Our Father is Royalty, which makes you Royalty. You are seated at the King's table. You belong to a Kingdom of Royalty. This is the promise of inheritance when you gave your "YES" to Jesus Christ. You are a Queen. Walk in your royal authority. Speak as if you know that you belong to royalty. You belong to a Royal family of believers and you have inherited all of the promises that come with it. This promise is for your children and your children's children, your seed. I challenge you to get with God and to find out what your promises are in Him.

WHAT AM I GRATEFUL FOR TODAY?

_____

_____

_____

WHAT IS MY GOAL FOR TODAY?

_____

_____

_____

PRAYER: Father God, thank You for including me in Your Kingdom of Royalty. Thank you that I have inherited the promised of being a Queen in Your Kingdom. Father I pray that You will reveal my promises to me that I may live in expectation of them. In the name of Jesus, Amen.

ADDITIONAL PRAYER:

_____

_____

_____

Day 6:

"I AM FORGIVEN"

"I am forgiven" means that I no longer feel offense toward anyone, and I no longer count the flaws or mistakes of myself.

Say it and write it 3 times:

1. _____

2. _____

3. _____

SCRIPTURE: Matthew 6:14 (AMP) "For if you forgive others their trespasses [their reckless and willful sins], your heavenly Father will also forgive you. But if you do not forgive others [nurturing your hurt and anger with the result that it interferes with your relationship with God], then your Father will not forgive your trespasses."

BONUS SCRIPTURE: Matthew 18:21-22 (AMP) "Then Peter came to Him and asked, "Lord, how many times will my brother sin against me and I forgive him and let it go? Up to seven times? Jesus answered him, "I say to you, not up to seven times, but seventy times seven.""

THOUGHT: God calls us to forgive others that He may forgive us. No matter what someone says or does, we are called to forgive that person seventy times seven, allowing God to do the work. Yes, that is a lot of times to forgive (LoL!). We are not inclined to allow the offender to cause further damage but we can still love them and at least say a prayer for them in hopes that they will heal. Remember, "hurt people hurt people". And most importantly, forgive yourself. If God can love us unconditionally and we are already forgiven, why can you not forgive yourself? When you become aware of a mishap be quick to forgive, release it to God, repent of any thinking or wrongdoing and pray for the other person involved.

WHAT AM I GRATEFUL FOR TODAY?

_____

_____

_____

WHAT IS MY GOAL FOR TODAY?

_____

_____

_____

PRAYER: Father God, please forgive me for anything that is not of you in my heart and I thank You for Your forgiveness. Thank you for allowing me to forgive anyone that has done anything wrong towards me, whether past, present or future. I release all of it to You. I pray in moving forward in forgiving, that I will be quick to forgive anyone that offends me and quick to love no matter what. That I will be slow to speak in response, processing the offense and slow to anger when I have experienced an offense. And most importantly Father, I will forgive myself for any past, present or future offenses that I hold myself hostage to. Please remind me when I have my moments of offense, of Your forgiveness for me. In the name of Jesus, Amen.

ADDITIONAL PRAYER:

_____

_____

_____

DAY 7:

"I AM PEACE"

"I am peace" means that I am free from disturbances and everything is quiet and tranquil around me.

Say it and write it 3 times:

1. _____

2. _____

3. _____

SCRIPTURE: John 14:27 (AMP) "Peace I leave with you; My [perfect] peace I give to you; not as the world gives do I give to you. Do not let your heart be troubled, nor let it be afraid. [Let My perfect peace calm you in every circumstance and give you courage and strength for every challenge.]"

THOUGHT: Jesus left His perfect peace for you. You have the power and authority to quiet any storm in your life. You are not obligated to stand still and just take whatever the storm throws your way. Do not be afraid and do not allow your heart to be troubled when the storms of life come. They may seem intense, heartbreaking, painful and may even seem like you feel like you aren't going to make it through the day but remember our God is

BIGGER. He has already settled the matter because He already knows our beginning and ending. Have the peace of God to go through the process, to get to the other side of the storm. The storms in life come to grow and mature us and are for us to help someone else through theirs.

WHAT AM I GRATEFUL FOR TODAY?

_____

_____

_____

WHAT IS MY GOAL FOR TODAY?

_____

_____

_____

PRAYER: Father God, thank you for your perfect peace. I thank you that Your perfect peace resides on the inside of me. I pray that when the storms of life come, I will be more inclined to draw from Your perfect peace and know the way of peace. I know that I will make it through the storm because You say that it has already been done. In the name of Jesus, Amen.

ADDITIONAL PRAYER:

_____

_____

_____

DAY 8:

"I AM FEARLESS"

"I am fearless" means that I fear NOTHING!

Say it and write it 3 times:

1. _____

2. _____

3. _____

SCRIPTURE: Isaiah 41:10 (AMP) "Do not fear [anything], for I am with you; Do not be afraid, for I am your God. I will strengthen you, be assured I will help you; I will certainly take hold of you with My righteous right hand [a hand of justice, of power, of victory, of salvation]."

BONUS SCRIPTURES: 2 Timothy 1:7 (NKJV) "For God has not given us a spirit of fear, but of power, love and a sound mind."

1 John 4:18 (NKJV) "There is no fear in love; but perfect love cast out fear, because fear involves torment. But he who fears has not been made perfect in love."

THOUGHT: What are you afraid of? God is love. There are no punishments in Him. When you learn of God's love for you, you will not fear any punishment or anything outside of His love for you. Be engulfed in His love so much that fear has no way in. Fear is not of God. It is of the adversary, Satan. Anything that is done in fear has an absence of God's love.

WHAT AM I GRATEFUL FOR TODAY?

_____

_____

_____

WHAT IS MY GOAL FOR TODAY?

_____

_____

_____

PRAYER: Father God, I thank You that I have been made perfect in Your love that fear cannot exist. I thank You for Your strength, Your power and for You giving me the courage to be fearless. I know that You are with me in everything that I do. I know that You will seek justice for me when facing persecutions. I believe that there is no fear in Your perfect love. In Jesus' name, Amen.

ADDITIONAL PRAYER:

_____

_____

_____

DAY 9:

"I AM DEBT FREE"

"I am debt free" means that I am no longer obligated to pay or repay for my past mistakes. I owe no man anything but love.

Say it and write it 3 times:

1. _____

2. _____

3. _____

SCRIPTURE: Matthew 6:12 (KJV) "And forgive us our debts, as we forgive our debtors."

THOUGHT: I do acknowledge that we all have bills to pay and we owe on our homes, cars, investments, etc. But this is more so directed towards people. You owe no one anything but to love him/her. People will hold grudges thinking that someone owes them something when really it has nothing to do with you. If you made a promise, keep your word and if you are not able to keep your word, at least make it known so that there are no issues. You are to be a woman of your word. When it comes to being "debt-free", if anything we owe our Father EVERYTHING but He said that we are already debt-free because Jesus paid the ultimate price for us.

_____

_____

_____

_____

_____

_____

PRAYER: Father God, I thank you that I am debt-free in You. I thank You that my debts have been forgiven and paid for through the blood of Jesus. If there is anyone that I am holding in debt to me, I release them to You and ask that You forgive me. Your Word says that my debts are forgiven when I forgive my debtors. I owe no one anything but to love him/her. In Jesus' name, Amen.

ADDITIONAL PRAYER:

_____

_____

_____

DAY 10:

"I AM LOVE"

"I am love" means that I feel a deep affection for myself first, and then for my brothers and sisters.

Say it and write it 3 times:

1. _____

2. _____

3. _____

SCRIPTURE: Matthew 22:37-39 (NLT) "Jesus replied, "You must love the LORD your God with all your heart, all your soul, and all your mind. This is the first and greatest commandment. A second is equally important: 'Love your neighbor as yourself.'"

BONUS SCRIPTURE: 1 John 4:19 (TPT) "Our love for others is our grateful response to the love God first demonstrated to us."

THOUGHT: His love for you is unconditional. God is love and you were created in the image of God. That means that "YES", YOU ARE LOVE! A walking, talking, example of God and His love here on earth. Our relationship with God is very imperative. In order to love our neighbor, we have to first know how to love ourselves from God.

When we can love ourselves and see ourselves how God sees us, then we can better see and love our neighbor the way that God sees and loves them. Allow God to embrace you, flooding you with His eternal love. Then allow that love to resonate onto others. When you are grateful for His love, you will respond to your neighbor in that same love that was given to you.

WHAT AM I GRATEFUL FOR TODAY?

WHAT IS MY GOAL FOR TODAY?

PRAYER: Father God, I thank you for making me a walking, talking, loving being. I thank you that I am able to love my neighbor the way you have loved me. I pray God that You will direct me towards anyone today and forward that needs Your love. I believe that I am called to love the way you have loved me, unconditionally. In Jesus' name, Amen.

ADDITIONAL PRAYER:

_____

_____

_____

DAY 11:

"I AM LIGHT"

"I am light" means that wherever I go, I illuminate and ignite the atmosphere.

Say it and write it 3 times:

1. _____

2. _____

3. _____

SCRIPTURE: Matthew 5:14-16 (TPT) "Your lives light up the world. Let others see your light from a distance, for how can you hide a city that stands on a hilltop? And who would light a lamp and then hide it in an obscure place? Instead, it's place where everyone in the house can benefit from its light. So don't hide your light! Let it shine brightly before others, so that the commendable things you do will shine as light upon them, and then they will give their praise to your Father in heaven."

THOUGHT: You are the light in God's eyes. He looks at you with such adoration, compassion, and love in His eyes. You were created to be the light to share His love with others, to illuminate any room or place that you walk into bringing the light of God's love to it. Your light is important as there are many that are anticipating to receive your light.

Are you hiding? If so, it's time to come out and be the light that God has called you to be in this world.

PRAYER: Father God, I thank You for Your light. I thank You for creating me to be a light to someone's eyes. I thank You that I have power and authority to change atmospheres because of Your light. I pray that on my daily journey You will lead me to cross paths with the people You want me to share my light with. In Jesus' name, Amen.

ADDITIONAL PRAYER:

_____

_____

_____

DAY 12:

"I AM PROTECTED"

"I am protected" means that I am covered and shielded from any damage or destruction.

Say it and write it 3 times:

1. _____

2. _____

3. _____

SCRIPTURE: Psalms 91:1-3 (TPT) "When you sit enthroned under the shadow of Shaddai, you are hidden in the strength of God Most High. He's the hope that holds me and the Stronghold to shelter me, the only God for me, and my great confidence. He will rescue you from every hidden trap of the enemy, and he will protect you from false accusations and any deadly curse."

THOUGHT: Many times, we feel that we need to protect ourselves by defending our own honor. When you honor God, He will honor you. So, no need to protect yourself, He will honor you by protecting your honor as it is a reputation of Him. We exhaust ourselves of all energy, stressing ourselves to prove to others who at the end of the day still cannot comprehend. Why? God is and has always been your protection. Protected from some things you already know and many unknown.

When it comes to people, you no longer have to protect yourself by defending yourself. Easier said than done, right? Allow God to defend you. He is always and forever in control of ALL things. Utilize the Word of God and prayer. Use that to fight and let God fight for you. You no longer have to prove yourself to anyone but just be who you are in Him. God has the final say! Allow Him to be your protection against the nonsense and drama of others.

WHAT AM I GRATEFUL FOR TODAY?

_____

_____

_____

WHAT IS MY GOAL FOR TODAY?

_____

_____

_____

PRAYER: Father God, I thank You that I am protected by You. I thank You that You protect me from harm every day. My honor, reputation, everything that may be misunderstood by others is all in You. You know and understand me better than anyone else. When I am feeling discouraged by others and the urge to protect and defend myself comes, please remind me of Your strength, that it is greater. I will hide beneath Your wings of Your shelter and allow You to protect my reputation. In Jesus' name, Amen.

ADDITIONAL PRAYER:

_____

_____

_____

DAY 13:

"I AM FREE"

"I am free" means that I am no longer controlled or held in bondage to anyone or anything.

Say it and write it 3 times:

1. _____

2. _____

3. _____

SCRIPTURE: Galatians 5:1 (TPT) "Let me be clear, the Anointed One has set us free-not partially, but completely and wonderfully free! We must always cherish this truth and stubbornly refuse to go back into the bondage of our past."

THOUGHT: You are free from sin because of Jesus. You are no longer in bondage of your past, present and future. You are free from other people's thoughts, opinions, anything that is not who God says you are. You are free to be who God called you to be! You're no longer obligated to fit into someone else's box of who they think you are or should be. You are free from your past. Those things that you may not be proud of, leave them in the past. If God has forgotten your past, why are you still living in it? Whatever your past may consist of, no matter how harsh, bad or crazy you may think it is, it is all null and void and no longer exist today! God still loves and adores you. Be free and live in the freedom that God has called you to.

WHAT AM I GRATEFUL FOR TODAY?

_____

_____

_____

WHAT IS MY GOAL FOR TODAY?

_____

_____

_____

PRAYER: Father God, I thank You that You have set me free from my past, present and future sins. I will no longer allow my past to keep me in bondage. I will no longer allow anyone to keep me bound to my past. I thank You that I am free from people and their opinions. I will no longer live to please others but live to please You God. You are and will always be pleased with me, even when I'm not in alignment with Your Word. I pray that I will always and forever meditate on the goodness of who You say I am so that I will not live to be a slave of my past. In Jesus' name, Amen.

ADDITIONAL PRAYER:

_____

_____

_____

DAY 14:

"I AM HEALED"

"I am healed" means that I am free from any and all disease and injury. I am perfect, whole, and complete.

Say it and write it 3 times:

1. _____

2. _____

3. _____

SCRIPTURE: Isaiah 53:5 (NLT) "But he was pierced for our rebellion, crushed for our sins. He was beaten so we could be whole. He was whipped so we could be healed."

THOUGHT: You are physically, mentally, and emotionally healed. Jesus paid the price for you to be healed on the cross. His blood was shed for you to be whole (mind, soul, and body) in Him. You have been restored to your original health, which is perfect, whole, and complete in Him. There is no sickness, disease, or mental illness in Him. Doctors, people and the ways of this world may want to label you to fit into their box so that they can feel better about comprehending you. God has the last say and He says that you are healed! His Word is more powerful! Believe today that no matter the challenge, whether physically, mentally, or emotionally, God has already healed you. Live from that place of healing by walking as if whatever it is that you struggle with no longer exists. Continue to trust God's word, meditating on it, believing until He reveals the change in you. This doesn't mean that you stop taking medication (if applicable). It means that you trust God for your healing, allowing Him to make the change for you.

WHAT AM I GRATEFUL FOR TODAY?

_____

_____

_____

WHAT IS MY GOAL FOR TODAY?

_____

_____

_____

PRAYER: Father God, thank You that You have already healed me. Thank You for restoring my health to its original state. I believe that You have not called me to lack anything when it comes to my well-being. I am healed in You, mind, body and soul. I pray that You will give me the strength to work on myself in any and all areas that You call me to be healed. And I pray that You will lead me to the right person/people that will help me be in good health. In Jesus' name, Amen.

ADDITIONAL PRAYER:

_____

_____

_____

DAY 15:

"I AM FAITH FILLED"

"I am faith filled" means that I completely trust God. With strong convictions I trust and believe all of His Words.

Say it and write it 3 times:

1. _____

2. _____

3. _____

SCRIPTURE: Hebrews 11:1 (AMP) "Now faith is the assurance (title deed, confirmation) of things hoped for (divinely guaranteed), and the evidence of things not seen [the conviction of their reality-faith comprehends as fact what cannot be experienced by the physical senses]."

BONUS SCRIPTURE: Hebrews 11:6 (TPT) "And without faith living within it would be impossible to please God. For we come to God in faith knowing that he is real and that he rewards the faith of those who passionately seek him."

THOUGHT: Whatever it is that you are believing God for by faith, believe and know that it is done. Align the Word of God with whatever it is that you are believing Him for. Study the Word of God, declare and decree those scriptures that line up with what you are believing God for over your life and walk in it by faith as if it is already done until you see it manifested in your life. Whether you're believing God for a spouse, a child, a house, a new job, a saved loved one, wealth, whatever it may be, there is a scripture for it. He heard your prayers and He is answering them. Allow God to work things out in His perfect timing. Some answers come quicker than others. Do not be discouraged. God is in the background working things out on your behalf. God wants to give you the desires of your heart. Believe and know that God will come through for you and He is always right on time.

WHAT AM I GRATEFUL FOR TODAY?

_____

_____

_____

WHAT IS MY GOAL FOR TODAY?

_____

_____

_____

PRAYER: Father God, I thank You for answered prayers. I thank You that You have already given me the desires of my heart. I know that I cannot please you without faith in believing that there is no prayer that is impossible. I trust You. I believe in You for all things. I believe that all things are possible through You. I will stand on Your Word believing that if You did it for others in the Bible You can surely do it for me. In Jesus' name, Amen.

ADDITIONAL PRAYER:

_____

_____

_____

INTERMISSION

Are you still there? Good! You made it halfway through! Awesome! But now isn't the time to fully celebrate, nor to slack. You still have more work and you don't have much longer to go.

Do you feel a change on the inside? Do you see a change in how you see yourself? Are you aware of the love that God has for you and basking in that love? Prayerfully you do, you are and you can feel the light illuminating on the inside of you.

Keep going … you've got this!

DAY 16:

"I AM PATIENT"

"I am patient" means that I remain steadfast and unmovable despite opposition and difficulty that come my way. I trust God for my breakthrough.

Say it and write it 3 times:

1. _____

2. _____

3. _____

SCRIPTURE: Hebrews 10:36 (AMP) "For you have need of patient endurance [to bear up under difficult circumstances without compromising], so that when you have carried out the will of God, you may receive and enjoy to the full what is promised."

BONUS SCRIPTURE: James 1:4 (NKJV) "But let patience have its perfect work, that you may be perfect and complete, lacking nothing."

THOUGHT: Patience is a fruit of the Spirit (Galatians 5:22) that definitely takes time to cultivate. You have to go through some things in order to truly understand and grasp being patient in the trials of life. There are trials that you have already experienced and trials that you have yet to continue to experience on your journey of life. Know that when you are experiencing the trials of life you are perfect and complete in Him, lacking nothing. He knew that the trial would come. He has prepared you and equipped you on the inside to overcome. Get into His thoughts through prayer so that you will be able to get through the process. He will assure you and give you peace to get through to the other side of the trial. Your testimony will be for someone else later in helping them get through to the other side of their trial.

WHAT AM I GRATEFUL FOR TODAY?

_____

_____

_____

WHAT IS MY GOAL FOR TODAY?

_____

_____

_____

PRAYER: Father God, thank You for giving me patience to endure through the trials of life. I thank You that my trials aren't just for me but for others to share my testimony in overcoming them. I thank You that I am perfect and complete, lacking nothing as I endure. I know that You will guide me as I depend on You for direction through the process. In Jesus' name, Amen.

ADDITIONAL PRAYER:

_____

_____

_____

DAY 17:

"I AM BEAUTIFUL"

"I am beautiful" means that I am pleasing to the senses and mind. I am held at a very high standard. I am wonderfully made.

Say it and write it 3 times:

1. _____

2. _____

3. _____

SCRIPTURE: 1 Peter 3:3-4 (TPT) "Let your beauty come from your inner personality, not a focus on the external. For lasting beauty comes from a gentle and peaceful spirit, which is precious in God's sight and is much more important than the outward adornment of elaborate hair, jewelry, and fine clothes."

THOUGHT: You are beautiful just the way you are. True beauty lies in your heart and it radiates from the inside out. God created you with a beautiful heart. When God looks at you, He is in awe of your beauty, admiring you, His creation. We can look at ourselves in the mirror and see our imperfections through our natural eyes, whether physically or morally, but have you asked God to show you yourself through His eyes? I challenge you to look in the mirror and admire your own beauty with His eyes. Ask God to show you what He sees. Embrace your beauty and be comfortable with the imperfections while here on earth. We all have them and it is what makes us all uniquely different. But when God sees you, there are no imperfections. Why? Because there are no imperfections in His Kingdom. You were beautifully and wonderfully created!

WHAT AM I GRATEFUL FOR TODAY?

_____

_____

_____

WHAT IS MY GOAL FOR TODAY?

_____

_____

_____

PRAYER: Father God, I thank You that I was created beautifully in Your sight, inwardly and outwardly. I thank You that in You I have no imperfections. So, I embrace all of who I am and who You created me to be. I pray that on those days I may not see how beautiful I am in You, that You will give me Your eyes to see my inward beauty that it will radiate on the outside. In Jesus' name, Amen.

ADDITIONAL PRAYER:

_____

_____

_____

DAY 18:

"I AM REDEEMED"

"I am redeemed" means that I have been purchased at a price that I could not afford. I have been repaired, restored, and set free from the consequences of sin.

Say it and write it 3 times:

1. _____

2. _____

3. _____

SCRIPTURE: Ephesians 1:7 (NKJV) "In Him we have redemption through His blood, the forgiveness of sins, according to the riches of His grace..."

BONUS SCRIPTURE: Psalms 107:2-3 (TPT) "So, go ahead-let everyone know it! Tell the world how he broke through and delivered you from the power of darkness and has gathered us together from all over the world. He has set us free to be his very own!

THOUGHT: Yes!!! Let anyone and everyone know that you have been redeemed by God through the blood of Jesus. Darkness no longer has a hold on you! God doesn't hold you in bondage to your past, to your sin. That is the enemy! Your past has been washed away, wiped cleaned and you are created in the newness of God. If you don't know who you are in Him, I challenge you to seek Him to find out. There are great and wonderful things that He wants to show you. Things that He wants you to accomplish that will be a blessing to not only you but your children, family, friends, anyone that is connected to you. You no longer have to settle for being ordinary. God created you to be extraordinary in Him.

WHAT AM I GRATEFUL FOR TODAY?

_____

_____

_____

WHAT IS MY GOAL FOR TODAY?

_____

_____

_____

PRAYER: Father God, thank You that I have been redeemed from my past sins (past, present, and future) through the blood of Jesus. Thank You that You do not hold me bound to my past and that it no longer exists in You.

I pray that when the enemy tries to come and remind me of my past, that I will not fall prey to His lies but will be reminded of Your redemption for me. The enemy has no power over my life. I have been washed clean and belong to You. In Jesus' name, Amen.

ADDITIONAL PRAYER:

_____

_____

_____

DAY 19:

"I AM VICTORIOUS"

"I am victorious" means that I have already won.

Say it and write it 3 times:

1. _____

2. _____

3. _____

SCRIPTURE: 1 Corinthians 15:57 (AMP) "but thanks be to God, who gives us the victory [as conquerors] through our Lord Jesus Christ."

THOUGHT: The battle has already been won! You have the V-I-C-T-O-R-Y!!! You have the VICTORY! There is no battle bigger than God. When the storms of life come, tell them that your God is bigger and that "it" has already been defeated. Do not allow the things of this life to stress you out or make you feel like you are less than. And don't allow it to make you feel like you have been defeated and have no power. Rest in Him and stand in His peace. You have power and authority to walk in your victory. Speak it and claim it! You have already won!

WHAT AM I GRATEFUL FOR TODAY?

_____

_____

_____

WHAT IS MY GOAL FOR TODAY?

_____

_____

_____

PRAYER: Father God, I thank You that I already have the victory to overcome the storms of my life. I thank You that You are bigger than my storms. I will rest in Your peace and strength to overcome the storms of life. There is no such thing as defeat in You. I pray that when I cannot hear you or feel You with me in the storm, that I will stand knowing that You are with me, that You never left me and that the battle is already won. In Jesus' name, Amen.

ADDITIONAL PRAYER:

_____

_____

_____

DAY 20:

"I AM AN OVERCOMER"

"I am an overcomer" means that I have successfully conquered any and all problems and difficulties.

Say it and write it 3 times:

1. _____

2. _____

3. _____

SCRIPTURE: 1 John 5:4-5 (TPT) "You see, every child of God overcomes the world, for our faith is the victorious power that triumphs over the world. So who are the world conquerors, defeating its powers? Those who believe that Jesus is the Son of God."

THOUGHT: You are an Overcomer! You have overcome the traumas, disappointments, pain, hurts, alcohol, drugs, promiscuity, sufferings (whatever applies), any and all things that this world has to offer that isn't of God. Jesus overcame them all! He defeated this world already. Your faith is what has sustained you until this day. You can stand in your faith and power of being an overcomer. No one or nothing in this world can take anything away from you unless you allow it to. You have control over the choices that you make. As an overcomer, you stand over the storms of life not in them. As an overcomer you are able to help others overcome by sharing your testimonies.

WHAT AM I GRATEFUL FOR TODAY?

_____

_____

_____

WHAT IS MY GOAL FOR TODAY?

_____

_____

_____

PRAYER: Father God, I thank You that I am an overcomer. I am grateful that as Your child, You have already given me the victory to overcome the things of this world through Your Son Jesus. I am not bound by the things or ways of this world. In my heart is your peace which sustains me. I pray God that as an overcomer, You will put people in my path that I may help them overcome the things of this world. In Jesus' name, Amen.

ADDITIONAL PRAYER:

_____

_____

_____

DAY 21:

"I AM UNIQUE"

"I am unique" means that there is no other like me. I am one of a kind.

Say it and write it 3 times:

1. _____

2. _____

3. _____

SCRIPTURE: 1 Peter 2:9-10 (MSG) "But you are the ones chosen by God, chosen for the high calling of priestly work, chosen to be a holy people, God's instruments to do his work and speak out for him, to tell others of the night-and-day difference he made for you-from nothing to something, from rejected to accepted."

THOUGHT: There is only one "You" here on this earth. You were uniquely created, the good, the bad, the ugly, to stand out from the rest. There is only one person with your name and DNA, that can only do what God created you to do here on this earth. You are the only one that has the intelligence, "know how", charisma, experience and the skills of what God has called you to do. Have you ever felt like you didn't belong or fit in? Don't take it to heart. God was setting you apart.

Apart from the things that would hinder who you are in Him and what He has purposed you for. God didn't want you to fit in. He wanted you to stand out from the rest. Don't look at it as a negative but that you are a light, chosen to represent His Kingdom. You were once considered nothing to this world, rejected by humanity because you didn't do what others were doing, following the crowd. You are accepted first by God and there are people that accept you because of the light that you bring to this world. You may or may not have come into contact with them yet. Know that your light, that something on the inside of you will attract those that will receive and accept you for you.

WHAT AM I GRATEFUL FOR TODAY?

_____

_____

_____

WHAT IS MY GOAL FOR TODAY?

_____

_____

_____

PRAYER: Father God, thank You for choosing me and setting me apart. Thank You that I was uniquely created to be me. That there is only one me in the world that can do what it is that You need me to do. Now that I know that I am set a part for Your purpose and will for my life, I will no longer look at it as a negative but as a blessing. I will embrace my uniqueness. I pray that many will be drawn to Your light in me and that they may receive salvation. In Jesus' name, Amen.

ADDITIONAL PRAYER:

_____

_____

_____

DAY 22:

"I AM BLESSED"

"I am blessed" means that I am content, enjoying good pleasure and fortune.

Say it and write it 3 times:

1. _____

2. _____

3. _____

SCRIPTURE: Psalms 84:12 (AMP) "O LORD of host, How blessed and greatly favored is the man who trust in You [believing in You, relying on You, and committing himself to You with confident hope and expectation]."

THOUGHT: You are blessed and greatly favored putting all of your trust and reliance in God for all areas and things pertaining to your life. God wants to bless you beyond your wildest imagination. His desire is for you to have an expectation of nothing but goodness from Him. It pleases Him to see you pleased and enjoying happiness from His blessings. He wants to bless you in every area of your life and not just in the areas that you only trust Him with. You are blessed to be a blessing to those that are connected to you. God says to trust Him and He will open the windows of heaven and pour you out a blessing so much that you cannot contain. Your cup will run over, blessing others from your overflow. Whatever area of your life you are expecting God to bless you in, believe that it is already done!

WHAT AM I GRATEFUL FOR TODAY?

_____

_____

_____

WHAT IS MY GOAL FOR TODAY?

_____

_____

_____

PRAYER: Father God, thank You for calling me blessed. Thank You for blessing me to be a blessing to others. I will put all of my trust in You. I believe that You want me to be blessed in every area of my life. I believe that You want to bless me with the desires of my heart. I pray that I will trust the timing of Your blessings for my life and that I will not be discouraged or doubtful in how my blessings will be manifested. I trust and believe that there is nothing impossible for You to do. In Jesus' name, Amen.

ADDITIONAL PRAYER:

_____

_____

_____

DAY 23:

"I AM A VIRTUOUS WOMAN"

"I am a virtuous woman" means that I am righteous. I exhibit moral excellence.

Say it and write it 3 times:

1. _____

2. _____

3. _____

SCRIPTURE: Proverbs 31:10 (AMP) "An excellent woman [one who is spiritual, capable, intelligent, and virtuous], who is he who can find her? Her value is more precious than jewels and her worth is far above rubies or pearls."

THOUGHT: When God created woman, He perfected man. He gave women everything that the man lacked and more. I'm not saying that women are better than men because when God created man and woman, He created them to be equal. What I am saying is that you have a virtue that is priceless, far from what any man can offer. Far beyond what a man can compensate for. It cannot be brought. There is no amount of money that can compensate for what God has created in you. You do not need to lower your standards to fit into anyone else's box. You ought to think of yourself with high esteem. Walking as the virtuous woman that you are, walking in excellence. There is no competition. You have your own lane and only compete with the person you were last year, month, week, and yesterday. Embrace yourself and have standards that are worthy to be respected.

WHAT AM I GRATEFUL FOR TODAY?

_____

_____

_____

WHAT IS MY GOAL FOR TODAY?

_____

_____

_____

PRAYER: Father God, I thank You for creating me to be a virtuous woman. I thank You for making me a woman of value that is priceless. I am thankful for the morals and integrity you have instilled in me. That I may walk in high regards no matter what my past looks like because You created me in excellence. I pray that You will continue to lead me, guide me, and show me how to walk with integrity and value for myself. In Jesus' name, Amen.

ADDITIONAL PRAYER:

_____

_____

_____

Day 24:

"I AM LIVING"

"I am living" means that I am actively full of life, full of vigor, and thriving.

Say it and write it 3 times:

1. _____

2. _____

3. _____

SCRIPTURE: Galatians 5:25 (TPT) "Since we live by the Spirit, let us keep in step with the Spirit."

THOUGHT: You are a living, breathing, speaking spirit of God, processing a soul that dwells in a temporary house known as your body. Your spirit was created in the likeliness and image of God, His heart. His Spirit lives in you. God wants you to live from your heart, in spirit as this is the true experience with Him. He wants to communicate with you directly. You can draw from and rely on His love, peace, joy, and strength (to name a few) living from the Spirit. This is true life and living in God. Every day you awaken, you have another day to experience living from within His Spirit. He will direct your path giving you direction for your day. Be present and opened to what His Spirit is saying to you each day. He is waiting for you, wanting to tell you things, answering questions and dropping knowledge on your daily experiences. He is protecting you from danger that may be ahead or putting you in the path to be blessed or a blessing to someone. Live from a place of openness to Him and you will be living from a place of true gratitude and thankfulness. Be led in spirit by His Spirit and experience true living.

WHAT AM I GRATEFUL FOR TODAY?

_____

_____

_____

WHAT IS MY GOAL FOR TODAY?

_____

_____

_____

PRAYER: Father God, I thank You that I am alive and living, that Your Spirit lives in me. I thank You that I have direct access to You and You can hear my thoughts before I speak them to You. I trust that You already have the answers to any and all pertaining to my life. I pray that I will be in tune to Your Spirit every day that You are guiding me on my daily journey and I will be open and present to receiving You. In Jesus' name, Amen.

ADDITIONAL PRAYER:

_____

_____

_____

DAY 25:

"I AM FRUITFUL"

"I am fruitful" means that I am abundantly productive in all that I put my mind and hands to.

Say it and write it 3 times:

1. _____

2. _____

3. _____

SCRIPTURE: Leviticus 26:9 (NKJV) "For I will look upon you favorably and make you fruitful, multiplying you and confirming My covenant with you."

THOUGHT: Everything you put your mind and hand to in God, He will make fruitful multiplying it. This is His promise to you and confirmation of His covenant with you. God wants to make you fruitful in birthing not only physical babies but spiritual ones as well. Whether its ideas, creations or starting a business, He will make it fruitful and multiply. You cannot be fruitful without God. At least not the way that He has purposed you to be. Relying on others can be a letdown if you are putting your sole trust in them and not God. Would you rather be fruitful your own way and receive the crumbs off the table or be fruitful His way, receiving the whole loaf of bread? You should never have to compromise yourself or your abilities, limiting yourself in anything. God's fruit is limitless and His multiplication are eternal. Your fruit will leave a legacy lasting for many generations to come.

WHAT AM I GRATEFUL FOR TODAY?

_____

_____

_____

WHAT IS MY GOAL FOR TODAY?

_____

_____

_____

PRAYER: Father God, I thank You that I am called to be fruitful and multiply. I am thankful for Your covenant promises to me and that whatever it is that I put my mind and hand to that is purposed in You, that it will be fruitful and multiply. I am creating a lasting legacy in You for generations to come. I pray that I will trust Your leading with the ideas, dreams and imaginations of my mind that You give me and that You will give me the resources to accomplish these things. In Jesus' name, Amen.

ADDITIONAL PRAYER:

_____

_____

_____

DAY 26:

"I AM A MOTHER"

"I am a mother" means that I give birth in the natural and spiritual realms. I provide, nurture, and protect.

Say it and write it 3 times:

1. _____

2. _____

3. _____

SCRIPTURE: John 16:21 (AMP) "A woman, when she is in labor, has pain because her time [to give birth] as come; but when she has given birth to a child, she no longer remembers the anguish because of her joy that a child has come into the world."

THOUGHT: Whether you have natural children or not, you are still a mother. You have spiritual babies that you have birthed already or that are waiting to be birthed through you. God has given you seeds that are being watered in your journey of life. The hardships and sufferings cultivate your baby. And just like in the natural when you don't know the exact time a baby is to come but can only prepare for the due date, you birth your spiritual baby in whatever current situation you're in. Your baby can come earlier than you predicted or can come later than expected. It may or may not feel like the right time but God always knows best. Know that your pain and sufferings in life are not in vain. You are giving birth to something that will help someone else on their journey.

WHAT AM I GRATEFUL FOR TODAY?

_____

_____

_____

WHAT IS MY GOAL FOR TODAY?

_____

_____

_____

PRAYER: Father God, I thank You that I am able to give birth to the spiritual babies that You have entrusted to me. I thank You that as a spiritual mother, I have children in the spirit and natural realm that can benefit from me. Whether I have children of my own or not, I was called to give birth to the ideas, creations, and innovations that You have impregnated me with. I pray that You will put me in the path to be able to pour into those that may need a motherly figure. In Jesus' name, Amen.

ADDITIONAL PRAYER:

_____

_____

_____

DAY 27:

"I AM A WIFE"

"I am a wife" means that I am a partner with God first in marriage. I am a help mate.

Say it and write it 3 times:

1. _____

2. _____

3. _____

SCRIPTURE: Ezekiel 16:8 (NKJV) ""When I passed by you again and looked at you, indeed your time was the time of love; so I spread My wing over you and covered your nakedness. Yes, I swore an oath to you and entered into a covenant with you, and you became Mine," says the Lord God."

BONUS SCRIPTURE: Song of Solomon 2:16 (NKJV) "My beloved is mine, and I am His…"

THOUGHT: Whether or not you are wife already in the natural, you belong to the Lord first. You have a covenant with Him that cannot be broken. He is your covering. He is the one that loves you with a love that no man can give unless that man first knows and loves the Lord for himself. And even then, he still might not come close. When you gave your life to Christ, you were claimed as the

Bride of Christ. The blood of Jesus seals the covenant between the two of you. You are His and He is yours. He has an oath to keep, a promise to you for all that you are entrusting Him with. Whether you are already a wife, seeking or waiting to be a wife, you are already a wife in Christ. You are His partner first, His helpmate, His "baby's mama" giving birth to His spiritual babies. In learning to be His wife first, He is preparing to be the wife for the husband you're purposed for (for the woman that seeks to be a wife).

WHAT AM I GRATEFUL FOR TODAY?

_____

_____

_____

WHAT IS MY GOAL FOR TODAY?

_____

_____

_____

PRAYER: Father God, I am thankful to be Your wife, Your partner, Your "baby's mama", Your beloved bride. As I am waiting to be married, I first get to learn from You. Whether I decide to marry, remarry or to stay single, I am always and still your wife first. I pray that as You prepare me to be a wife (or for the woman that is already a wife), that You will give me the tools, knowledge, understanding, patience and love for my future husband. In Jesus' name, Amen.

ADDITIONAL PRAYER:

_____

_____

_____

DAY 28:

"I AM A SISTER"

"I am a sister" means that I am a fellow comrade, sharing similarities with other women, and bonding with sisterhood connections.

Say it and write it 3 times:

1. _____

2. _____

3. _____

SCRIPTURE: Philippians 2:2 (TPT) "So, I'm asking you, my friends, that you be joined together in perfect unity-with one heart, one passion, and united in one love. Walk together with one harmonious purpose and you will fill my heart with unburdened joy."

THOUGHT: Whether you have a biological sister or not, you have sisters in Christ. If you aren't connected, get connected! Our connections are to bless one another. Our strengths and weaknesses balance one another. I know that there can sometimes be friction amongst the sisterhood unit, but don't let it stop you from connecting. Connect with women that are going to love, support, challenge you to be better, encourage and give you Godly sound guidance and advise. If you are connected to women that are judgmental and always have something negative to say, it's time to reevaluate and change your circle. We all have differences and we are to embrace one another loving in unity, celebrating one another's victories and accomplishments. Get in where you fit in and if not, build your own table of women that have the same heart and interest.

WHAT AM I GRATEFUL FOR TODAY?

_____

_____

_____

WHAT IS MY GOAL FOR TODAY?

_____

_____

_____

PRAYER: Father God, I thank You for my divine connection to my sisters. I thank You that You have given me women that love, support, and challenge me to be better. I thank You that You have surrounded me with women that see the best in me and love me from that place. I pray that my heart will always be opened to receive another woman in spite of our difference. I know that we are to be a blessing to one another. I pray that You allow me to see how I can be a blessing to my fellow sister and how she can be a blessing to me. In Jesus' name, Amen.

ADDITIONAL PRAYER:

_____

_____

_____

DAY 29:

"I AM HOPEFUL"

"I am hopeful" means that I FULLY trust God and I am confident that He will fulfill my desires and expectations.

Say it and write it 3 times:

1. _____

2. _____

3. _____

SCRIPTURE: Psalm 42:5 (TPT) "So then, my soul why would you be depressed? Why would you sink into despair? Just keep hoping and waiting on God, your Savior. For no matter what, I will sing with praise, for living before his face is my saving grace!"

THOUGHT: Be hopeful about your future. Tough times are only temporary and they serve to teach us and grow us. Whether you're hoping for a better life, marriage, dating life, career, education, way of living, etc. Whatever it is that you are hoping for, trust and know that God is going to bring it to pass in His perfect timing but it starts with you and the way you see and think about it. While you're patiently waiting, praise Him in the midst! Work on you. Grow and mature and prepare for whatever it is that your heart desires. This is what will keep you focused and in Him. Praise Him in the midst of it all. When you begin to start focusing on the thing you are hoping for, it can be a bit discouraging because you see that you are still without. Begin to praise Him and thank Him for what is already done and this will put you back into alignment.

WHAT AM I GRATEFUL FOR TODAY?

_____

_____

_____

WHAT IS MY GOAL FOR TODAY?

_____

_____

_____

PRAYER: Father God, I thank You that I can put my hope and trust in You about my future. You know all things and You know what my heart is desiring. I thank You for giving me the desires of my heart when I put You first and trust that it is already done. I will forever continue to praise you for this is my saving grace! In Jesus' name, Amen.

ADDITIONAL PRAYER:

_____

_____

_____

DAY 30:

"I AM WOMAN OF PURPOSE"

"I am a woman of purpose" means that I was intentionally created by God to be a vessel used by Him to execute His will here on earth.

Say it and write it 3 times:

1. _____

2. _____

3. _____

SCRIPTURE: Romans 8:28 (AMP) "And we know [with great confidence] that God [who is deeply concerned about us] causes all things to work together [as a plan] for good for those who love God, to those who are called according to His plan and purpose."

THOUGHT: God had purpose for you before you were even created. You are here on this earth for His purpose and plan for your life. I know it can get a bit confusing because we tend to think we are here for ourselves. And yes, some people are and never get to experience the true intent of their being. When you gave your life to Christ, you were realigned to His purpose for your life. The purpose that was originally intended. What a time to be alive right now! Who are you? What is your purpose? What does God want you to accomplish her on earth? If you don't know, now would be the time to seek Him and find out. I promise, He has something great that He wants to share with you. You are a woman of purpose. You are here for a reason and that reason is between you and your Father in heaven.

WHAT AM I GRATEFUL FOR TODAY?

_____

_____

_____

WHAT IS MY GOAL FOR TODAY?

_____

_____

_____

PRAYER: Father God, I thank You that I am a woman of purpose. I thank You that You have created me to accomplish something in this earth. I pray that You will speak to me, give me clarity on my purpose in You. I pray that there be no confusion distracting me from Your purpose for me. I am determined to live every day on purpose! In Jesus' name Amen.

ADDITIONAL PRAYER:

_____

_____

_____

CELEBRATION AND REFLECTION

Congratulations! You made it through the Infinite Love 30-day devotional journey! WOOOHOOO! Now you can celebrate! I'm so excited for you because I know that you are thinking and speaking better about yourself then you were when you first started on day one. You are more mindful of yourself and how God sees you. You feel more aware of your self-value, self-worth and most importantly, self-love.

This 30-day journey was all about you learning the love of God and how He sees you. For you to take on that mindset and see yourself how He sees you. By now, it should come natural to you. And if it doesn't, you can do this journey over and over again until it does. Anytime a negative thought or anyone or anything comes against who God says you are, you can speak the truth, reminding your mind of what God says about you. Don't be deceived by the lies of the enemy! Proverbs 23:7 (The Passion Translation) says, "For as he thinks within himself, so is he." Whatever you think of yourself, that is what you are. In your thinking, you produce your own reality of who you say you are.

And whatever you believe about yourself, you will attract. You have the POWER to produce a positive reality!

In sharing my journey, I can only hope that it has helped you to see who you are in Him. You can now walk in your divine authority of who the Divine Creator says you are. Every day you became stronger. Every day you became more and more aware of your value. You became more aware of the Divine's voice. That soft spoken, loving voice that spoke nothing but positive words of encouragement to you. Even when you may have not gotten it right, He still spoke loving and kind words to you. There is nothing in this world that you can do to change how God loves and sees you. You are so loved way beyond what you can imagine or think.

I pray that in moving forward, you will make this a continuous part of your life's journey. It can be doing the 30-day devotional journey yearly, quarterly, or monthly. Invite others to join the journey with you and you all can encourage one another as you go along. Allow your fellow sister to speak into your life, and you into hers. Have fun with the journey! And even if you don't need to journal, you can still have a conscious mindset on a daily basis. Whatever you feel that you may need to work on for that day, whatever you feel that you are lacking, you can speak a positive word of affirmation that comes into alignment with what God says about you, define the word for yourself so that you will know what you are speaking over your life, the thought behind it, think of something you are grateful for in that day, make a goal for the day, and to say a prayer, thanking God for who He says you are. Remember to always seek the Word of God in your journey. It's a part of the journey. His Word will become illuminated in your thinking. Revisit your past journaling to track your progress and to see how far you have come. We are growing and learning every day. Always remain a student of life. This life here on earth is nothing but a learning place, a place of preparation for Eternity. Much love to you and many blessings!

www.ingramcontent.com/pod-product-compliance
Lightning Source LLC
Chambersburg PA
CBHW072200090426
42740CB00012B/2331